Original title:
The Comfort of Familiar Recipes

Copyright © 2024 Creative Arts Management OÜ
All rights reserved.

Author: Victor Mercer
ISBN HARDBACK: 978-9916-94-342-7
ISBN PAPERBACK: 978-9916-94-343-4

Mug of Memories

In a trusty mug, I sip my tea,
Each gulp a giggle, oh so free.
Grandma's secret, a dash of spice,
Why does it taste like toast or rice?

From noodle soups to cookies baked,
Chasing memories, no journey faked.
Each recipe holds a tale so bright,
As I recall, I laugh with delight.

A Broth of Belonging

Stirring the pot, a wild affair,
I toss in laughter and pinch of care.
A broth of garlic whiffs through the air,
My cat thinks it's dinner—oh, how unfair!

The kitchen's a circus, a true comedy,
Where veggies dance in perfect harmony.
Chef hat on, I take my stance,
Recipe flops? I'll take a chance!

Flavor-Filled Journeys

A dash of chaos, a heap of cheer,
Flavor-filled journeys bring friends near.
With herbs and giggles piled on high,
Baking blunders? We all just sigh.

From pesto pasta to dessert divine,
Counting mishaps, oh, what a line!
Each taste a memory, savored with glee,
Who knew flour fights could set us free?

Spoonfuls of Love

In the kitchen, a mess takes shape,
Flour flies, oh what a drape!
Sugar spills, and eggs go crack,
Laughter echoes, no turning back.

Cookies burn, but spirits bake,
Recipe calls for fun, not fate!
Mixing bowls and silly songs,
In this chaos, where heart belongs.

Timeless Delights

Grandma's tales in each ingredient,
A dash of joy, pure exuberant.
Salt and sugar, dance around,
Making magic, that's profound.

Potatoes twirl in buttery cheer,
Chopping onions brings a tear!
Sizzling pans with cheerful whir,
Dinner's ready, let's not deter!

Memories in the Mixing Bowl

A pinch of laughter, a scoop of grace,
Whisks flying in a wild embrace.
Spatulas dancing, it's quite absurd,
Recipes shared without a word.

Each taste tests a happy past,
Flavorful bytes, they never last.
From burnt bread to perfect pie,
With each meal, our spirits fly.

A Recipe for Togetherness

Chop the veggies, don't make a mess,
This cooking gig, a fun-filled test!
Add a sprinkle of silly fun,
Stirring joy, 'til we're all done.

Dinner prep with goofy faces,
Messy hands in a race of races.
Eating first, cleaning up last,
With each bite, we're free at last!

Ingredients of Home

In the kitchen, chaos reigns,
Flour flies like some wild rain.
A pinch of salt, a splash of glee,
Mom's old apron fits just me.

The blender's on, it roars like a beast,
Trying to mix my midnight feast.
Burnt toast sticks, oh what a sight,
But laughter fills the air tonight.

Flavorful Memories

Grandma's cookbook, pages stained,
Every recipe, a laugh retained.
Cookies and cakes, a sugary dance,
Whisking away at every chance.

The oven beeps, a joyful sound,
Each dish stirs memories profound.
Anise and cinnamon fill the air,
While we retell stories with flair.

A Dash of Tradition

Noodles tangled like old yarn,
Mom swears they'll win the dinner war.
Tomato sauce like a messy art,
Who needs a plan? Just follow your heart!

The family gathers, forks in hand,
Slurping loudly, oh isn't it grand?
With every bite, a chuckle shared,
In tasty moments, no one is scared.

Savoring Yesterday

Leftovers hide like treasures rare,
Finding them feels like a dare.
A spoonful here, a forkful there,
Each bite whispers, 'You were there!'

A feast of yesterdays piled high,
With flavors bold that never die.
In scattered meals and silly sighs,
Old recipes bring laughter's rise.

Recipes of Resilience

When life hands you lemons, just make some pie,
Throw in sugar and egg, give it a try.
A dash of the silly, a splash of the sweet,
Who knew baking was a dance with your feet?

When pots start to bubble and pans start to clatter,
Embrace kitchen chaos, it doesn't matter.
Stir in some laughter, sprinkle on cheer,
In every mishap, find joy and a beer!

Nurtured by Flavor

Grandma's old apron, a treasure so fine,
Twirled in the kitchen, we dance to divine.
Her secret concoction, like magic, it steams,
In the cauldron of memory, we stir up our dreams.

With each little nibble of pancake delight,
A flip gone wrong turns into a flight.
Maple syrup's sticky, it glues us with glee,
Who knew breakfast could taste this carefree?

Nostalgic Nibbles

Crumpets and cookies, crumbs on the floor,
Laughter erupts as we constantly pour.
The blender protests as the chaos unfolds,
But through all the mayhem, pure joy it molds.

Cookies with sprinkles stacked high in a tower,
Tip them too fast and you'll feel the power!
A sprinkle, a squish, a crash—and a laugh,
In this circus of flavors, we always find half.

Holding onto Heritage

With dusty old cookbooks piled high on the shelf,
We gather round tables, just being ourselves.
A pinch of your secret, a scoop of my grace,
It's dinner theater—everyone's in the race!

From sauces that bubble to cakes that won't rise,
We taste our tradition, much to our surprise.
Each bite tells a story, a sprinkle of flair,
We laugh at the flops—this chaos we share!

Heirloom Flavors

In Grandma's kitchen, there's always a mess,
With flour on faces, it's quite a finesse.
Her secret ingredients, we ponder and chew,
It's mostly just love, and a pinch of taboo.

Mismatched spices dance in a clunky old jar,
Who needs fancy labels? We know who you are!
The taste of her stew makes the neighbors conspire,
While we laugh at her tales, fueled by heat and desire.

Stirring Sweet Reminiscence

A spoonful of chaos, a dash of delight,
Recipes scribbled in ink fade from sight.
When laughter erupts, and the oven's ablaze,
We bake up our memories in oh-so-fun ways.

Pasta that's tangled, and sauce that's too thick,
Every cooking disaster holds its own trick.
With a sprinkle of sugar and a slice of our past,
Each bite is a story, each nibble a blast.

Familiar Aromas

The scent of baked cookies wafts through the air,
It's a hug from the oven, I swear it's a prayer.
When mixing up batter, we dance with delight,
With flour in our hair, we don't care 'bout the sight.

Burnt edges remind us of lessons we've learned,
While "oops" seems too mild, for the cake that got turned.

Smiles and errant sprinkles cover the floor,
Oh, what joyous madness, who could ask for more?

Recipes Passed Down

This pie's baked with stories, a family lore,
With crusts made of laughter, who could ask for more?
Whisking our troubles, with each joyful beat,
In every sweet failure, we stand on our feet.

Great Auntie Ethel brought her version of fries,
The secrets she holds, a surprise in disguise.
From sauces to cakes, we all share a tilt,
In all of these memories, the joy is our quilt.

Culinary Connections

In the kitchen, chaos reigns,
A dance with pots, as love constrains.
Flour flies like little snow,
Mixing goodness, wouldn't you know?

Grandma's soup, a secret blend,
In every spoon, a story penned.
A pinch of laughter, a dash of fun,
We taste our past, well-done and spun.

Gathered in the Kitchen

Chopping veggies with clumsy grace,
A flying carrot, oh what a chase!
Dough on my nose, I'm quite a sight,
Yet in this mess, all feels just right.

Turn up the heat, it's time to stir,
Spices clash, no need to confer.
We laugh more than we bake or fry,
In this kitchen, the good times fly.

Relics of the Palate

Old cookbook pages, yellowed and torn,
Each recipe whispers, 'be not forlorn.'
Burnt toast tales and tales of cake,
Each disaster, a memory to make.

We gather 'round for a feast of flair,
With socks that clash and messy hair.
Laughter serves the finest course,
In these relics, we find our source.

A Plateful of Memories

Pasta twirls with a wink and a grin,
Sauce splatters like a carnival spin.
Throw in a meatball for good cheer,
This plate's a party, bring up a beer!

Cakes with frosting that rivals the sun,
Every bite's a giggle, oh what fun!
From childhood kitchens to now and here,
It's all delight, with a sprinkle of cheer.

A Melodic Recipe

Mix a dash of laughter, sprinkle some cheer,
Grab a bowl of giggles, let's dance without fear.
Add a heaping tablespoon of quirky delight,
Whisk it all together, oh what a sight!

Sizzle sounds of joy, bubble up some fun,
Chop the onions silly, till the tears come undone.
Stir in the stories we laughed about last week,
Bake those memories until they're golden peak!

Whiffs of Love Through the Air

A pinch of chaos, a splash of the past,
Smell the soup of laughter, forever it lasts.
Throw in some antics, not to be shy,
Those burnt cookies showcase our attempts to fly!

Sprinkle it here, oh what a mess,
How many eggs cracked? Well, we'll just guess!
But every mistake leads to giggles galore,
With a side of fond memories, who could ask for more?

The Heart in Every Ingredient

Grab a soup pot, let's concoct a dream,
Add some wild spices, like laughter and cream.
Measure out smiles, don't forget the zest,
Each spoonful whispers, this meal is the best!

Toss in a chuckle, sauté it just right,
Don't mind the mishaps, we'll laugh at the bite.
Pour in some mischief, serve it with flair,
For each bite we take, says, 'I truly care!'

Stirring Vintage Dreams

Stirring a pot filled with nostalgic fun,
Whisking up memories, one by one.
Fold in the laughter, a sprinkle of grace,
Taste the sweet moments, hold them in place!

A recipe for joy, a dash of the past,
With every soft cupcake, we're having a blast.
Churn out the silly, let's not be tame,
In this kitchen of dreams, we'll always feel fame!

An Invitation to Feast

Come join me for a dinner, oh so grand,
With flavors that will tickle, sure to withstand.
Pasta that dances, and spices that sing,
Each bite a delight, it's a culinary fling.

From grandma's old apron to the oven's warm glow,
One bite of her pie, and you'll surely know.
Chili so thick, it can stand on its own,
A spoonful of laughter, in each pot that's grown.

The Warmth of Well-Worn Cookbooks

My cookbook is weathered, stains everywhere,
Each recipe whispers, 'Don't you dare fear!'
Forget the fine dining, it's simple I seek,
Burnt edges and giggles, that's the real peak.

Flip through the pages, each dog-eared page,
A scribbled note reads: 'Just wing it, don't gauge!'
From burnt toast disasters to soggy soufflés,
In this messy kitchen, our joy always stays.

Savory Stories

Every meal has a tale, some funny, some sad,
Of when I'd forgotten to put in the rad!
The soup turned to jelly, a sight to behold,
But we laughed 'til we cried; that's how life unfolds.

A stir here, a dash there, a pinch for good luck,
My cake fell like magic; what terrible luck!
Yet with shared smiles and forks intertwined,
In every small mishap, great memories we find.

Gathering Around the Table

Gather 'round the table, the feast has begun,
Pastas, and curries, oh this will be fun!
We'll reminisce tales of the chaos we made,
From mishaps in kitchens to grand culinary parades.

As forks clink together, and laughter erupts,
We'll toast to our blunders, and all that it cups.
With each silly story, our hearts surely swell,
In this joyous embrace, there's magic to tell.

Cooking with Heart

In a pot I throw in spice,
Just a pinch, not think twice.
A dash of laughter, a spoonful of glee,
Cook up a storm, just wait and see.

Forgot the garlic? No worries, mate,
We'll call it 'air-fried' on a dinner plate.
With each small chop, I dance with delight,
Cooking's just chaos with a pinch of 'Alright!'

Burnt the toast? A breakfast trend!
Who knew charred edges could be a friend?
With coffee strong enough to wake the dead,
I smile wide, just shake my head.

So if your kitchen's a zany zone,
Just roll with the punches, you're not alone.
A recipe's just a guide to create,
So here's to cuisine, let's celebrate fate!

Legacy on a Plate

Gran's old cookbook became my muse,
With stains and rips, it gives me blues.
"Just eyeball it," she wrote with flair,
Yet I measure twice, while pulling my hair.

Cookies that spread like a painter's brush,
Try to bake them without a fuss.
"Secret ingredient?" A child's sweet grin,
Then crumbs of chaos where I once had thin.

Pot roast? It's a kind of magic trick,
In ten hours, it's a bit too slick.
With each tender piece that falls apart,
I taste my past, with all my heart.

So here's to dishes that tell our tale,
With laughs and messes where none can fail.
A pinch of this and a dash of that,
Mainly love served up on a satirical plat!

Hearthside Harmony

Gather 'round when I'm in the zone,
Dinner bells ring, it's like a cyclone.
Chopping veggies at a blurring speed,
Who knew my fingers were birth control for the need?

Stirring sauce is an artful fight,
Orchestrating flavors that don't feel right.
Twirling spaghetti like a dance so grand,
Just keep the fork and don't use your hand!

A recipe's a riddle dressed as a dish,
Follow directions? It's hard to wish.
But call me the chef of improvisation,
Serving laughs, not just a creation!

In this kitchen chaos, well-versed in jest,
We find our joy, we find our best.
So let's serve up goofy, seasoned with cheer,
A feast for the heart that's always near!

Comfort in Simmering Pots

A simmering pot is my favorite tune,
Whistling away, like a silly cartoon.
Chop and splash, what a grand mishap,
Cooking with joy, wear the chef cap!

Stirring fears with a wooden spoon,
Uneven slices under a complaining moon.
"Too much salt!" I hear them cry,
But a pinch of laughter will always comply.

Once, I tried soufflé to impress,
Flopped so hard, it's now a mess.
I serve it up with a wink and grin,
Dessert or disaster? Let the fun begin!

So in my kitchen, bold flavors collide,
With spices and giggles, I take great pride.
The secret's not just in what's hot,
But laughter and love in every pot!

Whisking Away Worries

In the kitchen, chaos reigns,
Eggs are flying, who knows where?
Flour fights back, the dog complains,
A cake might rise, with hopes and flair.

Butter's melting, oh what a sight,
Sugar's dancing, sweet ballet,
Mix it all with all your might,
Just pray the smoke alarm won't play.

A splash of joy, a dash of fun,
Spatula winks as it joins the fray,
Perfect mess? It might be done!
Who cares? Let's roll the dough and sway!

Every flub becomes a treat,
When laughter's baked in every bite,
Worries whisked away, oh sweet,
What joy to be a chef tonight!

A Canvas of Comfort

Pasta tumbles with comic grace,
Noodles slip, and sauce takes flight,
A splash of red, a silly face,
Dinner's done with sheer delight.

Pickles dance on the counter's edge,
As I search for fresh ingredients keen,
My cooking skills? They're on a ledge,
But this chaos? It tastes like a dream!

Garlic's laughter fills the air,
Tomatoes giggle, onions cry,
Each bite surely shows I care,
Just wish the dishes would comply!

Yet through the mess, the love will show,
Every meal is a work of art,
In this kitchen, laughter's flow,
Each spoonful warms the weary heart!

Time-Honored Dishes

Mom's old cookbook, pages worn,
Spills and stains, a laugh-filled tale,
Each recipe, a bond reborn,
And yet that jello wiggles pale!

Stirring pots with glee and dread,
What's this spice? A mystery,
A pinch of laughter, just ahead,
What's next—an exploding soufflé?

Granny's cookies, charcoal gray,
But somehow they still taste just fine,
Do ovens have a goofy play?
Because they turn sweet into brine!

Yet with each mistake, love grows tall,
Old dishes keep our spirits bright,
Each laugh a thread in life's great hall,
Creating joy with every bite!

Heartfelt Helpings

Ladle lifts a hearty stew,
Splashes dance with silly flair,
Why is it green? I haven't a clue,
The cat just stares, gives me a glare.

Chopping veggies, keeping score,
But the knife slips, oh what a sight!
Alarming sounds—a culinary war,
Yet laughter bubbles, pure delight!

A charred roast becomes a joke,
"We meant it crispy, right?" we say,
And every meal, with laughter stoked,
Turns into fun, come what may!

So here's to all the heartfelt meals,
With memories that taste like cheer,
In every slice, a story peels,
As smiles linger, year after year!

A Feast of Familiar Faces

In grandma's kitchen, there's always a fight,
Who gets the last cookie? Oh, what a sight!
A spoonful of chaos, a sprinkle of cheer,
Smiles and burnt toast, our laughter sincere.

A cousin who spills spaghetti with glee,
Splatters of sauce as we all drink tea.
A recipe book with pages all torn,
Each dish a memory, slightly worn.

With each clatter and clink, we sing and we sway,
Creating new traditions in our own funny way.
A feast of familiar faces around,
Where the oddest of flavors in laughter are found.

Gathering around Comfort

When the pasta boils, it bubbles with glee,
Mom sneaks a taste, and it's never just three!
Spaghetti on walls, oh what a great mess,
Cooking's a circus, but we love it nonetheless.

The salad's a jungle, can you spot the green?
Carrots like soldiers, standing so keen.
A pinch of good humor, a dash of fun,
Our dinner's a party, and it's only begun.

We gather around, and the strangest of sights,
A casserole brunch that could start food fights.
Laughing and munching till our bellies feel tight,
In the warmth of the kitchen, we delight in the night.

Tasteful Echoes of Home

There's a pot on the stove, and a cat on the chair,
A whisk in one hand, and flour in the air.
Dad yells for help, but he's covered in dough,
As mom rolls the pastry, the laughter will flow.

The cookies are burnt, but we eat with delight,
Each crunchy disaster, a soft heart in sight.
A table set wide with our quirkiest fare,
An echo of flavors that's hard to compare.

Our kitchen's a symphony of clinks and of clatters,
More fun than your average cookbook can patter.
We mix and we mingle, our hearts full and free,
A medley of memories, just taste and you'll see!

Embracing Flavorful Heritage

Oh, the great aunt's chili with secrets untold,
A dash of surprise, it's daring and bold!
Spices that tickle and dance on the tongue,
With stories of old when the family was young.

The recipe wrinkled, yet cherished and bright,
A road map to flavor, setting taste buds alight.
Pies cooling on windowsills, joyful displays,
Rolling big doughnuts, it's a glorious phase.

With every deliciously funny mishap,
We cherish our roots, in our culinary clap.
Laughter encircles as we nibble and bite,
Embracing the flavors that make our hearts light.

Nostalgic Whispers from the Oven

In the kitchen, joys arise,
Muffins doing little jives.
Grandma's secrets, floury hands,
Mixing chaos with grand plans.

Chocolate chips in cookie dough,
Dance around as if in show.
Burnt edges bring a hearty laugh,
Who knew toast could be a craft?

Spaghetti twirls like a ballet,
Sauce splashes bright, hip-hip-hooray!
Meatballs roll like tiny rocks,
Dinner's fun with silly knocks.

Oh, the bread that won't behave,
Yeast erupts, a gooey wave.
Familiar tastes that make us grin,
In these bites, we dive right in!

A Spoonful of Memory

A dash of spice, a pinch of cheer,
Stirring memories, year by year.
Whisking up grandma's green delight,
Minty tales in each bite.

Pancake mornings start with fun,
Flipping fluff like a wild run.
Maple syrup drips like gold,
Sweet moments never grow old.

Tasty tales from the past unfold,
Marshmallows float, a sight to behold.
Hot cocoa hugs us, cuddled tight,
Chocolate smiles throughout the night.

Lemon meringue, sweet and bright,
Has a frothy, fluffy fight.
And in the mess, we find pure glee,
Cooking's laughter sets us free!

Culinary Echoes

Echoes of laughter in the pot,
Sizzle and pop, a funny spot.
Chili bubbling with spicy flair,
We snicker at the smoke-filled air.

Goulash journeys, here we go,
With weird flavors in tow.
Noodles tangled like old friends,
The fun in cooking never ends.

Grandpa's stew, a comic tale,
Potatoes bobbing, like a sail.
Every taste a joyous surprise,
With each spoonful, we improvise.

Pizza nights with wobbly cheese,
Feeding the cat, "Oh, what a tease!"
Kitchen chaos—what a show,
With every bite, our laughter flows!

Secrets Simmering on the Stove

Secrets simmer, pots a'clatter,
Mom's old recipes—what's in the matter?
A sprinkle here, a splash right there,
Mysteries lie in the air.

Pickles dance in vinegar brine,
Jars popping lids, oh how they shine!
Family feuds o'er who can bake,
From kitchen tricks, new friends we make.

Nachos piled in silly ways,
Cheese just melting, a cheesy haze.
Saucy fingers, laughter reigns,
With every dip, we lose our brains.

Onion rings, a crispy cheer,
Bacon whispers, "I am here!"
Secret flavors we adore,
Each recipe brings us back for more!

A Tapestry of Tastes

In a pot, a dance unfolds,
Chopping onions, tears untold.
Sizzling pans and spices fly,
Mom's secret blend, oh me, oh my!

Flour clouds in the kitchen breeze,
Baking cookies, oh such tease.
Burnt edges, but who could tell?
Charlie's laughter rings like a bell.

Mixing sugar, salt, and spice,
Recipes butchered, but tastes are nice.
Grandma says, "Just a pinch more!"
While I'm wondering, is that a chore?

Dishes crash; a milestone learned,
Every mishap, a laugh returned.
With each bite, a smile's sewn,
In this tapestry, love has grown.

Sifting Through Memories

A pinch of chaos, a dash of fun,
Each spoonful whispers, "You've just begun."
Grandma's pie, a well-worn guide,
Instructions lost, but joy has pried.

Eggshells flying, what a sight,
Batter flinging, oh, what a fight!
In this chaos, we find our grace,
Nothing ever stays in place!

The blender roars, a wild beast,
Smoothies fly, like a breakfast feast.
"Did I add the salt or the sugar?"
"Oh no, it's time to call a bugger!"

With every flop, memories grow,
Laughter shared in the culinary show.
We sift through messes, never alone,
In these moments, we build our own.

Spice-scented Reminders

Cinnamon whispers in the air,
Mixing memories with love and care.
The mixer trembles with glee and fright,
It's baking time, hold on tight!

Chili splatters and a garlic cheer,
"Oops, I can't see!"—that pot's too near.
Sautéed dreams in a sauce so bold,
Laughter sings from stories old.

Stirring pots, we gauge with eyes,
Seasoned coaches, no need for lies.
Did it bubble? Does it pop?
Oh wait, the butter! Please don't drop!

With spice and giggles, we take our turns,
In this kitchen, every heart yearns.
Every recipe tells a tale anew,
With tangled joys, our love shines through.

Whispers of the Past

In the pantry hides a magic jar,
Dusty treasures from afar.
A pinch of nostalgia, a twirl of fate,
Who knew cooking could be this great?

Saucepan chatters, don't forget the lid,
Rumpus unfolds—oh, what a bid!
Things get messy, but we don't mind,
In the kitchen, true treasure we find.

Beyond the stove, a chatter of yore,
Mom recalls, "We've done this before!"
Floury faces, eager to please,
Every flop simply adds to our tease.

Stirring up laughter, blunders galore,
Each recipe's a laugh we adore.
In the whispers of meals long past,
We share our heart, and joy is cast.

Cozy Dishes

In the pot, a stew does bubble,
Throw in some carrots, spice, and trouble.
The cat eyes leftovers like a hawk,
While I perfect my weird dance walk.

Potatoes waving from the skillet,
Vowing to make the meal a hit.
A splash of sauce, a pinch of cheer,
Guess who's getting dinner here?

Noodles twirl like dancers grand,
With sauce so thick, it's like a band.
Topping it off with cheese - oh my!
A heart attack in every bite, pie in the sky.

Chocolate cake that sings to me,
How can this slice be calorie-free?
My diet's on hold for dessert's delight,
With every forkful, I take flight!

Comfort in Every Bite

I baked a loaf, it rose with pride,
But then it looked like a lopsided slide.
With butter on top, it shines so bright,
I still call it a win—what a sight!

Pasta went swimming, in water galore,
It tried to escape, with a slippery core.
A dash of garlic, herbs in the mix,
This noodle disaster gets me my fix.

Fried chicken cracks in a joyous sound,
While I chase crumbs all over the ground.
"Just one more piece," I whisper and plead,
This crispy crunch is my heart's true need.

Pies cooling on windowsill, oh what fun,
A slice leads to two, and I'm not yet done!
I'll launch a coup against any diet plan,
Who needs a plan when food's such a fan?

Entwined in Flavor

Last night I cooked a colorful dish,
A stir-fry that promised to grant my wish.
But veggies danced like they lost their core,
In my kitchen, it's a flavor war!

As my biscuits rose to newfound heights,
They looked at me like, "Are we alright?"
With jam piled high, they couldn't complain,
Each crumbly layer a flaky gain.

Soup that splashed, a colorful tide,
Carrots and peas on quite the ride.
It leaped in my bowl, "Come try me, dear!"
But my spoon hesitated in trembling fear.

Dessert case winks from the counter wide,
"Choose me, choose me!" they seem to bide.
With cakes and cookies on hand for the take,
Who knew cooking could feel like a high-stakes bake?

A Melange of Voices

A recipe calls from the kitchen shelf,
"Add a pinch of chaos, mix with your elf!"
My whisk is squeaking with glee and strife,
Creating a scene—for what is life?

Sizzling sausages sing with flair,
Lurking in grease, if only they care.
"More mustard, please!" my friend takes a bow,
As hot dogs juggle; we cheer them now!

A pizza spins like a dream tonight,
Topping it with everything - what a sight!
"Did you just use anchovies? Oh dear!"
But the laughter around is worth every tear.

With muffins exploding like fireworks light,
We gather around, making memories bright.
Each nibble and chuckle fills up the air,
In the dance of our kitchen, we've found our flair!

Whisked Away to Childhood

In the kitchen, pots make noise,
Mom's secret stash of old toys.
Flour flies like snow in the air,
Chocolate smudges, nothing to care.

Spoons tangled in a silly dance,
Dad's mustache, just take a chance.
Cookies burn, but laughter stays,
Childhood memories in such a haze.

Pizza dough launched to the ceiling,
The cat plotting its next stealing.
Trying to bake, but what's that smell?
Oops! That cake's an epic fail!

Yet amidst the fumbles and the mess,
Family bonds, we now confess.
From whisking dreams to baking pies,
In these moments, joy never dies.

Flavors That Embrace

Spaghetti nights, sauce on my chin,
Mom says, 'Eat up, let the fun begin!'
Garlic bread bouncing off the plate,
Whispers of flavor, it feels like fate.

Dinner table's a laughter show,
Oops! I just turned the chili to dough!
Everyone gasps, forks held high,
One big giggle, my oh my!

Baked beans that danced on a bed of rice,
Dad claims, 'They taste just like paradise!'
But mixed with soda? What a sight!
Burps echo, we hold on tight.

Taco night becomes a landslide,
Toppings spill, can't hide our pride.
Adventures wrapped in tortilla bliss,
Each bite a flurry, who could resist?

A Taste of Togetherness

Potato salad secrets, oh so stout,
Who knew mustard could spark that route?
The kid's table holds the brunt of fun,
Corn on our faces, oh what a run!

Pasta paired with silly songs,
Dancing forks where everyone belongs.
Salad tosses become epic feats,
Lettuce flying across our seats.

Granny's pie, a tarry mass,
Wobbly crusts, and everyone laughs.
"That's art!" she says, with a wink,
We're too busy to even think.

Bubbles rise in pot and pans,
Disaster afoot, but joy never spans.
Together we savor each messy bite,
In our kitchen, laughter's always bright.

Sentimental Soups and Sweet Remembrances

Grandma's broth, a fragrant hug,
"Just a pinch!" turns to a chug.
Carrots diving amidst the swirl,
Each spoonful brings a lovely twirl.

Noodles tangled, a slurping song,
We'd laugh so hard, couldn't be wrong.
Dad says, "That's the noodle's fate!"
A broth battle—now isn't that great?

Dumplings dancing, puffed and round,
What's in the mix? Surprises abound!
One bite too spicy, whoops, there's a tear,
But through the laughter, it's love we wear.

Sweet memories in every taste,
Lessons in laughter, never a waste.
As we sip from bowls, our hearts align,
In these cozy meals, love's in the brine.

The Scent of Home

In the kitchen there's a dance,
With pots and pans in a merry prance.
A pinch of this and dash of that,
Whisking chaos, where's the cat?

The oven hums a silly tune,
While I'm baking by the light of the moon.
Sprinkles fly like confetti bliss,
Oops! I forgot the list – how'd I miss?

Flour clouds like a snowy day,
I'm covered in white, can't find my way.
But oh, the aroma begins to tease,
Can't find the spatula, just a tease!

And when it's done, we all rejoice,
Who knew burnt toast could be my choice?
With laughter ringing in the air,
Home is truly anywhere, I swear!

Comfort in Each Bite

In the pot, things start to bubble,
I drop in spices with a whole lot of trouble.
The noodles dance like they're in a play,
And I just tripped! Are they supposed to sway?

The fridge door swings, and out pops cheese,
I swear it just winked – oh, if you please!
A dash of this and a smidge of that,
Time for a feast, let's have a chat!

The neighbors peek in, they smell the stew,
Little do they know, I burned it too.
But laughter is better than a Michelin star,
With all my mishaps, I'm still a bizarre!

With every bite, a silly grin,
Messy meals are where fun begins.
Who cares if the recipe's went astray?
Each bite brings joy – hip hip hooray!

Stirring the Soul

A whisk and a stir, a mix-up in luck,
I added salt, then a fumbled pluck!
Tasting my work, it's a curious blend,
Is that cinnamon? Or just a trend?

The cake is rising, or maybe it's sinking,
I can't quite say, I'm mischief-thinking.
A spoonful of giggles, a splash of delight,
My dessert's a fiasco, but oh, what a sight!

Pasta on the ceiling? That's just how I roll,
"Abstract art!" I claim; it speaks to my soul.
With every failed meal, we're in stitches,
Food may misbehave, but laughter enriches.

So here's to the kitchen, a carnival spree,
Where ruins become stories, just you wait and see.
A dash of this, a sprinkle of fun,
At the end of it all, we've surely won!

Kitchen Chronicles of Love

The clock strikes twelve, my pie's in a spin,
Who knew baking would lead to such din?
Sugar and laughter, it's quite a sight,
Flour fights break out during our bite!

We trade secret recipes in a giggle match,
"Your cookies are crunchy, mine's got a scratch!"
Stirring up tales of gastronomic woe,
Cuz burnt muffins are tales that always flow!

Potatoes are dancing, a lovely charade,
Chopping onions while wearing a blade.
From sizzling pans to the sounds of a sigh,
We share in the chaos as flavors fly high.

But in the end, it's more than the meal,
It's the joy of togetherness that we feel.
With every mishap, our hearts intertwine,
In our kitchen chronicle, love is divine!

Warmth in Every Whisk

With flour clouds and eggs in flight,
My kitchen circus, oh what a sight!
Whisking dough like it's a dance,
I trip on spills, but take a chance.

Spoon in sugar, a sprinkle of flair,
My dog waits patiently by the chair.
He knows the look when treats are near,
A kitchen mishap, he gives a cheer.

Baking cookies, I might overdo,
Looks like the batter needs a sneeze or two!
Each spoonful's magic, albeit a mess,
My laughter echoes, it's nothing less.

In the chaos, joys arise,
The taste of home, a sweet surprise.
With every recipe, a tale to weave,
Through joyous laughs, I can't believe!

Tastebuds in Time

A pot of sauce, a splash of spice,
A recipe card that looks like dice.
I stir with vigor, while wearing a grin,
A pinch of chaos mixed with din.

Grandma's words echo, "Don't be shy!"
But I drop the garlic, oh my, oh my!
Tomatoes scatter like they're in a race,
Tasting the memories, I'm losing pace.

Whisking up dreams I once outgrew,
Like burnt popcorn, they stick like glue.
Yet laughter bubbles in the fragrant air,
Who knew that burst would take me there?

Every nibble takes me back,
To summers stacked with laughter's track.
In this culinary time machine,
I feast on funny, flavor-filled scenes.

A Symphony of Savors

Chopping onions makes me wail with glee,
Cinnamon whirls in a wild spree.
With pots like drums, and spatulas in hand,
I conduct this feast, my own little band.

Flour fairy dust in the disco light,
I twirl and I twirl until the dough feels right.
Sugar sprites dance on the counter too,
Making cookies sing, in a joyful brew.

Melodic mixture, it starts to rise,
Time for a taste, oh what a surprise!
The orchestra plays, my tongue takes flight,
Savoring laughter in each delicious bite.

With friends around, we share the sound,
Of forks and knives as flavors abound.
In this kooky kitchen, where joy is clear,
Each note of flavor brings us near.

Embracing the Unfamiliar through Comfort

I peek at the fridge; a leftover mess,
What's this odd veggie? I guess, I guess!
Chop it, sauté it, stir it with flair,
Who knows? It might just take me somewhere.

A dash of this, and a sprinkle of that,
Tastes like adventure, in a funky spat!
The recipe's vague, but I'll give it a whirl,
Turning kitchen chaos into a swirl.

With mystery spices, I take a leap,
Like madcap knights, we roast and we keep.
Each bite's a puzzle, a giggle, a tease,
Who knew that dinner would come with a breeze?

Through every blunder, a flavor born,
When cooking feels like a wildest dawn.
Embrace the strange, let the laughter flow,
In my quirky kitchen, there's always a show!

The Art of Savory Memories

In the kitchen, chaos reigns,
Flour flies like winter's snow,
Grandma smiles, a mischievous grin,
Chasing me with dough-filled woe.

A pinch of this, a toss of that,
Spices dance like a wild parade,
Mixing laughter with the fat,
How many eggs? I'm still afraid!

Recipes scribbled on loose scraps,
A secret sauce we can't recall,
Did I add tuna? Maybe, perhaps,
Dinner's a game of culinary brawl!

With burnt edges and soups so thick,
We raise our forks, the table sings,
In every bite, a clever trick,
As we toast to our cooking flings.

Pantry Treasures

In the pantry, treasures hide,
Old cans tell tales of yore,
What's that smell? A fishy guide,
Or maybe an ancient cheese galore?

Pasta shapes that look like art,
Guessing dinners has its thrill,
A can of beans, a work of heart,
Nutrition's goals? Let's just chill!

Button mushrooms, overdue for fate,
How did you end up here, my friend?
Baking powder, you're kinda late,
But welcome back, let's make amends!

A surprise meal, what could it be?
Together we laugh, and hope, and bake,
Analyzing stew, a mystery spree,
Each bite's a laugh, every taste, a mistake!

Baking Bonds Across Time

Whisking eggs like I'm in a race,
Fluffy clouds of sugar rise,
Grandpa's apron's a baking cape,
He's creating magic with wise, old eyes.

Chocolate chips like gems of joy,
Splat! One lands on the dog's nose,
Giggles burst, a playful ploy,
As flour covers all, even toes!

Ovens battle like rival teams,
Scone vs. pie, who will prevail?
Recipes turn to hilarious dreams,
What's this smell? Oh, is that a fail?

Yet through the flops, our hearts unite,
For every flop, there's laughter too,
Baking bonds that feel just right,
Sweet memories rise like fondue!

Reinventing Family Legends

Mom's famous stew, a mystery blend,
What's in there? Three types of meat?
She just smiles, lets the rumors mend,
The dog's still alive? Let's take a seat!

A few stale crackers—perfect for toast,
   Add garlic, a sprinkle of cheer,
   Every mishap a culinary boast,
   Give it a taste, hold back a tear!

   Family recipes like secret codes,
I write them down, but they disappear,
Every time they're reinvented loads,
   No one's sure what's really here!

But we gather 'round with hopeful plates,
   Forks poised to taste the tales we tell,
   In the mix of love, weirdness awaits,
   Each meal's a legend—our tasty spell!

Timeless Flavors in Tender Hands

In grandma's kitchen, there's a dance,
The pasta flops, they say, 'Take a chance!'
With flour clouds that swirl so high,
And rolling pins that seem to fly.

The cookies burn, but we don't fret,
Sugar sprinkles, can't lose a bet.
Laughter bubbles in every pot,
Even if we forget what we've got.

A pinch of love, a sprinkle of fun,
Mix it up, and watch them run!
Spoons fly like planes, oh what a sight,
Dinner time's a playful fight!

Each taste a tale from long ago,
With every bite, a giggling show.
Through thick and thin, our kitchen thrives,
Where laughter boils in our family lives.

Heirloom Plates and Heartfelt Tastes

Granddad's stew, it's quite a mess,
He claims it's art, we just confess.
With a dash of this and a scoop of that,
We end up with something like a cat!

The salad's wild, the dressing's thick,
Mom's cute mistakes, oh take your pick!
Carrots dance, and onions sing,
Flavor chaos is our favorite thing!

A bowl of soup or a hearty pie,
Each recipe's a strange supply.
We stir our pot, and soon we'll find,
We're all a little one-of-a-kind.

From clashing spices to burnt bread,
Each mistake is a story fed.
With heirloom plates, we all partake,
In family feasts that make us shake!

A Dash of Yesterday

Oh snap! The doughnuts didn't rise,
I guess that's life—much to our surprise!
Flour on my nose and icing on my cheek,
In this crazy kitchen, we all feel unique!

Pasta's tangled, like my hair today,
But it's all in fun—who cares anyway?
Sauce splatters like confetti gone wrong,
Yet in each mistake, we still sing our song.

The recipe's hints are cryptic and small,
Yet we hustle in the hope that we'll have a ball.
Spatulas flying, pots start to clang,
A symphony of chaos, let the laughter gang!

So gather 'round for flavor's wild quest,
No dish is perfect, but they're all the best.
With every bite, a giggle erupts,
In our silly kitchen where joy interrupts.

Recipes Passed Through Generations

A cookbook passed down, sweet and worn,
Pages turn pale, and legends are born.
Chocolate chips dance in a hopeful bowl,
While grandkids giggle, 'This is our goal!'

Soggy pizza, but smiles all around,
We craft our meals with love unbound.
Every mishap is a badge we wear,
In floury realms, we've not a care!

Sticky fingers and messy hair,
Cooking together, what a fair!
Old-fashioned fumbles and quirky feats,
Each tasty venture is a family treat.

With whispers of wisdom from days of yore,
We cook and we laugh, always wanting more.
Through hearty dishes and flavors sublime,
Our recipes bond us, transcending time.

Flavorful Footprints

In the kitchen I dance with flair,
A sprinkle of chaos fills the air.
Flour on my nose and pots a-jingle,
My dog looks on, ready to mingle.

The recipe calls for a smidge of spice,
But five shakes later, it's looking nice!
Taste-testing bites with wincing glee,
This could feed an army—or just me!

A dash of sass, a hint of wit,
Mixing old tales, that's how I sit.
Time to burn toast, it's all in good fun,
Dinner's a circus, but I'm the one!

When laughter simmers, and joy won't cease,
Even the kitchen holds a feast of peace.
With every mishap, I learn and grow,
These flavor-filled footprints, a chef's soft glow.

A Pinch of Tradition

Mom's old cookbook, pages quite smudged,
She'd laugh when I'd cook, a recipe fudged.
With a cup of sugar and a gallon of cheese,
Culinary chaos—oh, what a breeze!

Her secret ingredient? A wink and a grin,
"Don't worry much, it's the fun that you win."
But when my soufflé turned into a flop,
We laughed 'til we cried, then headed for shops!

Stirring in stories, like broth in a pot,
Keeping traditions? I've surely forgot!
But every mistake just adds to the tale,
With burnt offerings, we'll surely prevail.

Now every feast feels like family lore,
With laughter and love, who could ask for more?
So here's to the moments we cherish like gold,
In a kitchen alive where our stories unfold!

Relishing the Familiar

My grandmother's chili, a legend in time,
Full of wild flavors and flavors sublime.
Yet somehow each batch tastes slightly amiss,
Was it the love or the cans that she kissed?

Pasta for dinner, sounds simple enough,
But I've got a knack for making it tough.
Adding salt five teaspoons too late,
Now it's a briny, gelatinous fate!

Baking brownies, my absolute fav,
But each time they come out a little bit grave.
"Excuse me, not burnt, just an earthy delight!"
"More cake, less soap," I proclaim with delight.

From each little blunder, a memory grows,
In mixing and measuring, hilarity flows.
So here's to the meals that bring chuckles and cheer,
With flavors remembered, they're never austere!

When Spoons Speak

Gather round, dear spoons, hear tales long untold,
Of kitchen adventures that never get old.
One spoon says, "Hey! Let's stir it up bright!"
Another replies, "Last time we took flight!"

The spatula grins, "Let's flip without fear!"
But I know from experience—disaster is near!
With bubbling potions and floury clouds,
Even the cat joins in, singing out loud!

A pinch of this, oh, what's that they say?
"Measure? Who needs it? Let's throw it away!"
So in pots and pans, our laughter will soar,
Next stop—dinner or a culinary war?

When spoons begin chatting, you know it's a sign,
That recipes morph into something divine.
With the silliness bubbling, the meal takes its shape,
In the comedy kitchen, we'll always escape!

Moments Measured in Sprinkles

In my kitchen, chaos reigns,
Flour flies like fluffy rain.
Eggs are cracked with great intent,
But half shatters, oh, what a event!

Mixing bowls get out of hand,
Spoons flying, what a band!
Sugar dances, a sweet ballet,
Turns the mess to a glorious day!

The timer dings, I jump with glee,
Burnt edges? Just part of me!
I top with sprinkles, make it right,
"What a masterpiece!" I shout in delight!

Friends arrive, and we all munch,
Laughter fills our cupcake brunch.
Each bite taken, a wink and nod,
Who knew baking was this odd?

Recollections in Every Slice.

Grandma's cookbook, a treasure chest,
Faded pages, it knows best.
I mix her magic, a pinch of love,
Stir it gently, like a turtle dove.

Chopping veggies, ninja style,
With every slice, I grin and smile.
A dash of chaos in every bite,
Cooking tales that feel just right.

Cakes that wobble, frosting that drips,
Going for perfect, yet here comes the slips.
"Was that a cup or maybe a spoon?"
I laugh, my kitchen turning into a cartoon!

Slices served, let the tales unfold,
Friends gather, oh, the memories sold.
When the kitchen becomes a symphony,
In every bite, there's pure harmony!

A Taste of Nostalgia

Digging deep in the pantry's maze,
I find old jars with a lovely glaze.
A recipe scribbled on a napkin there,
"Good luck," the note says, with a cheeky flare!

Boiling pasta, it starts to race,
Splashes of sauce, a messy embrace.
Who needs plates? We eat from the pan,
Twirl those noodles, that's the plan!

Baking bread, oh what a sight,
My dough's like a pet, out of pure fright!
Knead it, shape it, toss in the herbs,
Cooking sometimes feels like suburbs!

Friends pop by, with forks in hand,
We feast on meals that's been well-planned.
Stories mix with every bite,
Nostalgia served with a side of light!

Kitchen Whispers

Whispers of garlic waft through the room,
Spices dancing, dispelling the gloom.
Chopping onions turns into a play,
Tears or laughter? Who can say?

The microwave beeps, a little tune,
I dance like no one is watching, oh, what a boon!
Popcorn pops in joyous delight,
It's a crazy party, every night!

A splash of cider, I measure askew,
"Did I add three? Or maybe two?"
Cooking's a game, with rules all bent,
Creativity soaring, my chef's intent!

Dinnertime's laughter, what could be better?
With every dish, my heart's a go-getter.
In this food haven, I'm never alone,
Kitchen whispers, my favorite tone!

Signature Flavors

In Grandma's kitchen, a dance we do,
Flour on our noses, and a cat named Lou.
Mixing up chaos, a pinch of delight,
And somehow it's cookies that come out just right.

Eggs in the bowl, shells on the floor,
We giggle and jest as we make a big score.
Taste buds are tingling, anticipation's grand,
Who knew kitchen mayhem could go so unplanned?

The recipe's classic, with twists of our own,
Throw in some sprinkles, let's see how they've grown.
Laughter is the key ingredient, you see,
When meals are a mess, it's the fun that we plea.

Now those sweet memories stick like old goo,
Filling our hearts just as much as our stew.
Next time we'll bake, with a much better aim,
But chaos ensures it's a never-dull game.

Savory Echoes

In mom's warm embrace, with recipes old,
Spices clash wildly, stories unfold.
Did we measure that right, or is this a fate?
A dash of the nutmeg, we might need more plate!

A casserole bubbling with joy on the stove,
Trading our secrets, the true chef's trove.
But how did it burn? Oh dear, what a sight!
We didn't need charred, just edible bites!

Gather the cousins, the world's not so grim,
A feast of our fails, and we might just swim.
Mixing together, it's not just for taste,
But moments so silly, we'd never let waste.

In the end, it's love that softens the stew,
Even if sometimes the target's askew.
Each bite we share pulls us tighter in cheer,
With laughter our seasoning—delicious and dear.

Threads of Tradition

A pot of something bubbling with flair,
Tangled in memories, a slight mismatch there.
The recipe's stained, like stories we spin,
With each little blunder, we all dive right in.

Dinner together, but where's the right dish?
Not trying to please, just the hopes that we wish.
Missing ingredients, oh what could it be?
Just wait, when it's served, it'll probably flee!

From grilled cheese disasters to juicy pie fails,
Each culinary venture, the laughter prevails.
Nostalgia is whisked into each happy bite,
Even when dinner feels like an odd fight.

Tradition spins wildly, like dough in the air,
Flavors collide, leaving us all in a stare.
In quirks and mistakes, the merriment grows,
Because food's not just food, but the love that we show.

Taste of Togetherness

We gather around with pots and with plans,
Chopping and stirring, collaborating hands.
A recipe beckons, yet chaos is here,
When one says 'salt,' another hears 'gear!'

The veggies are flying, the pasta's a mess,
Whisking up laughter, a family express.
There's something so sweet in the peeling of skins,
When errors taste funny, let the feasting begin!

Now pudding's too firm, the cake's wanting air,
But nothing can stop us, not even despair.
We'll hoot and we'll holler at all that we've done,
Concocting odd flavors—it's not quite a bun!

Sitting around with our plates piled sky-high,
Recalling our antics, the reasons to cry.
With each silly bite, as we chuckle and chime,
In the taste of our joys, we'll savor our time.

Whisking Through Time

In Grandma's kitchen, flour flies,
Eggs bounce like frogs, what a surprise!
Batter splatters, laughter sighs,
Mixing chaos, sugar highs.

Spatulas dance, like they're in a show,
Mom's secret spice? We'll never know!
Chasing the cat with a rolling dough,
Kitchen adventures, go with the flow.

A pinch of nostalgia, a dash of fun,
Measuring cups turned into a gun!
The smoke alarm sings, we've just begun,
In this wild bake-off, we're never done.

Cookies in shapes that defy the norm,
Unicorns, dinosaurs, spreading the swarm,
Each strange creation, in the warm
Embrace of laughter, we find our charm.

Roots and Recipes

In the old cookbook, the pages are brown,
Stains from the sauce, my, what a crown!
Each recipe holds a bustling town,
Where every mishap gets passed around.

There's always a secret from Auntie Lou,
A recipe twist that's too good to chew!
A dash of this and a sprinkle of goo,
Perfectly odd but it's tried and true.

The more that we cook, the more we can mess,
Like boiling water in a dress shirt, I guess!
Strange combinations, we simply obsess,
Yet through every failure, we feel the bless.

Dinner disasters bring joy to the night,
With burned garlic bread that gives such a fright!
Yet everyone laughs, feeling just right,
In roots of our meals, we find pure delight.

Baking Memories

Smelly socks or cookies? Who knew?
When baking, chaos finds its way through!
Flour on faces, laughter too,
Mixing the old with something new.

Grandpa's pie crust? A puzzle to solve,
Like bending light, it helps us evolve!
We wrestle the dough, it's a dramatic devolve,
Yet in that laughter, our hearts all revolve.

Burned edges, oh say, not so fine,
But each bite of mishap tastes just divine!
With funny stories, they start to align,
In every sweet moment, memories entwine.

The kitchen's a stage, chaos our friend,
With every mishap, it's love we send.
Baking together, a joy that won't end,
In each funny story, our hearts we mend.

Family Flavor Profiles

Uncle Joe's chili? A mystery blend,
We urge him to share, he just pretends.
Teaspoons of laughter at family bends,
Each spoonful served, like playful trends.

Sister's bright salad? Only greens, please!
We wonder if she's trying to tease!
With candied walnuts, it's sure to appease,
Colorful dishes that aim to please.

Dad's burnt toast? It's a breakfast thrill,
Whole grain crunch with a serious skill!
It crumbles like fond memories, it's a chill,
Like stories we share, they linger still.

In every odd flavor, our love takes flight,
Where meals are a canvas of laughter and light.
A dollop of joy, the moments feel right,
Tasting the bond in every bite.

Milton Keynes UK
Ingram Content Group UK Ltd.
UKHW021951151124
451186UK00007B/185

9 789916 943427